THE ARCHANGEL SUTRAS

A coll

G

Archangel = the writer's name for Gouri Sadotra

Sutra = a rule or aphorism in Sanskrit literature, or a set of these in grammar or Hindu law or philosophy

DEDICATION

I dedicate this book to my mother, Mrs Usha Sadotra who patiently read everything I wrote over the years and told me time and time again to publish my poetry and my dad, DR KC Sadotra who funded me financially whilst providing moral support.

Text and footnotes registered copyright © 7th December 2015 Gouri Sadotra,
All rights reserved. This publication may not be reproduced, stored in a retrieval system or transmitted, in any form or by any means, electronic, mechanical, photocopying, recording or otherwise, without the prior permission of the publishers.

Typeset by Gouri Sadotra.

CONTENTS

ROMANTIC POEMS

Moonface..**13**

Soft kisses...**17**

Birdsong..**20**

Pre-raphaelite beauty................................**22**

The beloved..**24**

Estoppeled you..**25**

The lover or the beloved...........................**29**

Memories...**31**

The love letter...**33**

Imagination..35

The meaning of magic...............................37

Emotion: the vehicle of love.....................39

Writer's block..40

Day dreaming...41

In the subterfuge......................................42

Split second...46

Hallucination of love.................................47

That I love you..48

Falling in love..50

Your invisible presence..................51

Girls like me..................53

Flickering flame..................55

Jump start myself..................56

Egyptian eyes..................59

For I already know..................61

Mr Butterfly..................63

The sweetest smile..................65

Mutterings..................66

Kiss your face..................67

Fresh faced beauty..................69

Red raw lips..70

Love at first glance......................................71

Emotional fatality..73

Half in love..75

Eternity and a day......................................76

HORROR POEMS

Mythical creatures......................................78

Hellhounds...83

Self-perpetuating hatred............................87

Of taking tablets...90

Minds' eye..**91**

Invisible you..**92**

The voices from outside..............................**94**

Stone wall..**97**

Waiting for Angels..**100**

Weakness..**103**

Beware beautiful child................................**104**

Gnarled beauty..**106**

Citadel of the mind......................................**107**

Corrupting power...**108**

Othello and MacBeth...................................**109**

Adultery..**111**

Captive in your eyes..................................**114**

Self destruction..**116**

Of bruises..**117**

Alice in Wonderland................................**118**

Let the devil decide the details................**119**

Kill..**121**

Your heart's desire....................................**122**

MISCELLANEOUS POEMS

A prayer from the dying..........................**123**

Talking to the spirits of the ages............125

The little mermaid.......................................129

Your approval..131

Between purity and hygiene.....................135

Shakespeare's sister...................................137

Self-realisation..138

Childhood friends..140

Of children..143

Chess pieces...147

On books...148

Lawyers...149

Sun and Moon..................................**151**

Friends..**153**

Childhood memories...................**155**

Birds..**159**

A summers' day............................**160**

Love of humanity..........................**163**

Intelligence verses education...**165**

A young plant................................**167**

Frenemies.......................................**168**

Princelings......................................**169**

Food..**170**

Imagination..**172**

Wondrous child..................................**174**

India of my childhood.......................**176**

The song of the archangel................**181**

Genius..**184**

The best..**185**

Time..**187**

Mens rea..**188**

Angels...**189**

Silence the moon................................**191**

Smartness in appearance...........................192

Gene bank...194

Footnotes..195

ROMANTIC POEMS

Moon face

Shooting thunderbolts through a garland of stars
He flies on golden wings
On the golden wings of a messenger – Hermes[1]

Through the planets and beyond the solar system
far, far and away
Across a backdrop of total darkness where the
universe swallows itself up

Dodging black holes
Those mismanaged intergalactic[2] potholes
Designed to suck you in until you surrender
everything
Including your very own soul

A passing nod and a wave through Orion's belt[3]
Flies the messenger of the gods

The Archangel Sutras

He skips past Heavenly Bodies aglow[4] one and all

The winged messenger of the gods, nimble and fleet of foot

To surrender everything
Including the very sovereignty over himself
To his lady love
Whilst leaving a shining and shimmering trail
Of stardust behind and below

On dancer's feet he is as swift of foot as of tongue

And he brings a gift, he says, and
"The gift that I give to you is a gift of me"

And her moon-face was aglow with the reflection of love's innocence
In those delicious crystalline moments draped in togetherness

The Archangel Sutras

Her mane of hair was entwined in strands of dark light
With just a sprinkle
A sprinkle of stardust

And he speaks

"If I could steal a glance from the shadows of death
I would summon Shakespeare from the heavens
And I would bring him only to you to speak out his sonnets
Just to you
For you
You are everything
And I am merely the messenger
And this is my message of love to you"

"So I will summon a long list of stars
That twinkle in the night time skies –
To beg them to leave their constellations

The Archangel Sutras

For a while just to meet you
For they want to meet you"

"For I would sprinkle a path of stardust for you
To walk upon through the heavens and beyond
To hear a chorus of cupids sing their love songs"

"For I have a secret just one secret
That I have been keeping from you
I want to open up and let my secret out
For now it is no secret that I send no gifts
Only a message
And that is a message of love"
And that is the message from the Messenger Boy

The Archangel Sutras

Soft kisses

Are you the most beautiful woman in the world
That you can extract these reactions out of me?
He says to me

And I stand there hungry for your kisses
All doe eyed and delicate featured
And inanimate romantic actor

As you recite the tenderest tales of love
On glimmering glistening glittering gossamer[5] wings
As pale as a petal and as daintily as dewdrops dancing on the breeze

And I weep the tenderest tales of teardrops

For I believed you and I believed in you

The Archangel Sutras

Even before you said it
Even before you told me your truths

For you have a singular way of making me feel special
As you unfold the mysteries beneath mine eyes
Those eyes that grow comfortable seeing you only in dimmed lights

And then I lay soft kisses on your forehead to bid you good night

Soft kisses on your face to bid you on your way to sleep

And finally the softest kisses
An your mouth
To close the seal on my heart felt feelings
Of love and devotion buried deep within my heart

Gouri Sadotra

The Archangel Sutras

For you made me complete
And this I convey to you
As I bid you adieu
And I lay outstretched on my bedstead
As you weave your magic
All around my world and me

Birdsong

She comes to me in my dream state
Again and again I think of her
A silhouette[6] of herself
Beautiful and aloof
With tumbleweed curls
Cascading past her shoulders and down her back

At night when I am all alone
And in my wishes which I send out to the world
I bring her back to me on a magical imaginary
object d' art
A flying carpet that flutters past in my mind's eye
As I beckon her mirage closer and closer to me
For this is the obsession with her
That I keep close to my chest behind sealed lips
And eyelids closed tight like shutters
As if in the manic midst of an Andalusian[7]
summer heat wave

The Archangel Sutras

Then I open my eyes
It is morning and her image is gone
And I am back to deal with the drudgery of the world
And all that I am left with is
The lingering early sweet sounds of the birdsong
Belonging to the nightingales
That sing about our secret love
To all that care to listen
By serenading passersby with images and descriptions
Captured in my minds' eye
For they want to share my love with the entire world

Pre-raphaelite beauty

Shall I let you into a little secret about how I
imagined you to be?
A flame haired, Pre-raphaelite[8] beauty
Dressed in flowing robes
As if you just stepped out of a gilt framed
painting

Maybe it was the auburn flames
Erupting like Vesuvius[9] from your head
Or your pale powdered skin
Or your somewhat placid demeanour
Always in control of your measured movements
Or the beguiling half smile on you quizzical
Mona Lisa[10] lips
Always questioning and never satisfied with the
answer

For you, for you are beautiful
But there is more

The Archangel Sutras

Much more to them then just mere beauty

Tell me, how many men have approached you
With outstretched arms
Snatching scattered moments of happiness with
you
Like gathering all the rays of sunshine
Escaping from the electromagnetic spectrum[11]

And you frequently sigh and say
Why does beautiful have to be synonymous with
good
Can't beautiful be bad sometimes as well?

The beloved

Beloved my life belongs to you
Images of my love belong only to me
You are my world
And everything in it has meaning only
Because you gave it meaning
When you spent time giving meaning to those
Moments marked and measured
Within my small world

The Archangel Sutras

<u>Estoppeled[12] you</u>

You are so heartbreakingly beautiful
Yes it's my choice and that is how I choose to remember you
Isn't it just amazing how emotion can distort memory to re-create a new reality?
A new reality which exists in our minds' eye
What we want to see
We see
And what we don't
We choose to extinguish from our collective imagination

So finally it's true
How time plays tricks on us all
Both our friend to give us company when we are lonely
And our tormentor to torture us for our past mistakes.

The Archangel Sutras

I can feel my heart break in violent slow motion
With all of those confused emotions tumbling out
distorted and real simultaneously
And finally denatured[13] until they are no longer
true
To the heart that once belonged to you
I guess that means that I am no longer in love
with you

And now even if you want to
I won't ever let you sneak back into my heart
through the back door
Stealing my emotions and saying that they belong
to you
As you wait for my reaction
I won't forgive you as I won't be there
Now you are just as ordinary and lacklustre to me
as everyone else

As I refuse to see you any other way
For I have estoppeled you from ever saying those
words to me

Gouri Sadotra

The Archangel Sutras

You know which ones
The ones I once craved to hear
That you refused to say

Now you'll never get the opportunity to say them
to me
Especially if you want to
Because you thought that I would wait forever
But forever just ended a while ago
And there is no going back

There is no more waiting
There is no more wanting
There is nothing left
But you will be fine
As you have not invested anything emotionally
You have nothing to lose

You maybe sad for a day or two
But you will move on
And meet someone else
Because for you

The Archangel Sutras

Falling in and out of love
Is as easy as turning a tap on and off
You will be fine
Just fine
Men like you always are

The Archangel Sutras

The lover or the beloved

I will have to wait like all the rest
For my turn to come up
And I will wait gratefully for that one chance
Because I never thought that I would feel for
anyone any man ever again
But I do feel
I feel for you
I am alive once more

For who is more lucky
The lover or the beloved?
I have often wondered myself
To give or receive the gift of love
Is a rare blessing
To love or be loved
If you had a choice of either
Which would you choose?

And for many people

The Archangel Sutras

That is life's little conundrum[14]
For the truly blessed
Are those couples that have been bestowed
The blessing of both
To love and be loved
Its expression act and emotion
Is one of life's highest states
And to belong to be part of such a couple
Is to be considered to be truly fortuitous[15]

Memories

My tears were a delayed reaction
Because it was only years later
Years after you had died
Could I remember all the little things
That you said and did
That made me love you
Just that little bit more

All those moments forming memories
That bonds one person to another
With ties that survive and surpass even death itself
So much so that even the God of death, Hades[16],
Cannot untie one person from another

And so we all go to our death
With our souls linking arms with the past the present and the future

The Archangel Sutras

Because we live in the memories
Of our loved ones our near ones and forever dear ones

So even if you ever hated me even for a moment
I would still love you for all of the happy
moments that we shared
When you were alive

Not just in my head and in my heart
But in dimensions of time and space
When we co-existed simultaneously
Breathing in the same universe together

The love letter

She wants a love letter
She wants a love letter
So I will send her a rose petal
To my lady love
I will send a love letter
On a pale petalled rose petal
From a tender young briar rose
And I will send it floating in the breeze
To my lady love
For she, … for she is the most beautiful flower in the world

"Oh" said the briar rose
For she… for she
Was brighter than all of the blooms
In the mythical forest where she lived
"Oh, but that would be the death of me!"
Gasped the pink hued briar rose
"For his rapacious[17] love,

has all but devoured me!"
"Just so that he can have his kiss!"

The Archangel Sutras

<u>Imagination</u>

So you say that I live in my imagination
And I don't even carry a photograph of you
But let me tell you a little secret
Instead of carrying a photograph
I carry good memories of you

With visual dexterity[18]
And the blink of my eyelids
I can conjure up my beloved's portrait
Within my mind's eye
These are the little things
That I do that remind me of you

But that picture is fading
And fading like the moon
So I have to see you again and soon
To refresh my earlier memories of you
So that I don't forget that face
That I imprinted and embossed

The Archangel Sutras

As a moving image within me

So many times when I feel sad and blue
I simply close my eyes
And imagine sitting next to you
And in my dream I turn to you and say
"It's the little things that you say and do
That makes me realise that I love you"

The Archangel Sutras

The meaning of magic

I can never forget the meaning of magic
Because for me that meaning is you
Only you
For I suddenly understood
The myriad ways of love
The unforgiven
The unforgettable
The unforgivable
For that meaning was you
Always you
In every action
In every word
In every gesture
You insinuated an emotive thought process which reverberated[19] around my brain
And made its shocking maneuveres to my head
All the while causing myocardial infarctions[20] along the way
Is this the method of true love?

Gouri Sadotra

For it certainly was the madness

Emotion: the vehicle of love

When actions don't speak volumes
And when thoughts fail to translate
From the metaphysical into the metaphorical
When the glowing embers of love is alight
And flickers in full view in front of the whole universe.
Without words
Without action
And without thought
Emotion becomes the vehicle of communication
Translating all messages
From the lover to the beloved
And back again

Writer's block

I had stopped writing but then I met you and now
Whenever I see your face my head just explodes
with words
Words that fall haphazardly
Maybe even clumsily into sentences
Paragraphs
And finally into pages
Filled with poems
About every emotion and every feeling
Perhaps I emote too much
But that is the effect that you seem to have on me

Day dreaming

I go to bed thinking of you
I fall asleep dreaming of you
I wake up wondering if you are there

I spend my entire time wondering where you are
For you are on my mind always

In the subterfuge[21]

The very moment I realised that he was
cheating on me
My heart froze
And any feelings that I had for him
Evaporated

Now I am senseless
Numb even
Where he is concerned
I will never shed a tear over him again

Now for me he is nothing and no one
A nobody
Who has no legal personality within my
reality
He only exists in the marginals
In the subterfuge
That is society
That surrounds my life

The Archangel Sutras

For now his silence is golden as I do not want
to hear even one syllable from him ever again

His hateful smile
Mockingly forcing a new reality
How I hate him
Now his sweet mocking words
Making mockery of any love
And affection that he had towards me
Fill me with disbelief
Fill me with hatred

After all that he has done to me
Yet still he professes his love towards me?
It makes me realise that there is use for me
yet!
It makes me realise that I am still necessary
At least for a little while longer
At least until the next time
So don't try to talk to me ever again
For you know how to

Gouri Sadotra

The Archangel Sutras

Inflict hurt
Inflict harm
On a woman's seditious[22] heart
For you have drained the very happiness from within me

All that is left to do is to siphon[23] of all the hatred I hold for you
As my heart is sickened with sadness

And I want to silence you
I want to stop your mouth
I want to estoppel you
From ever saying those tender words to me ever again

Which words do you say?
I love you
I need you
I want to be with you
You are more important to me
Than my very own self

Gouri Sadotra

The Archangel Sutras

I live for you and I'd die for your love

Yes it is true
for I want to silence the moon from singing
its silver tongued sonnets of eternal love

Split second

For I fell in love with you in a split second
Because you are so fall-in loveable
But it would take eons[24] to fall out of love with you

And I want to keep you captive under my watchful gaze
Until you decide that you are finally ready to fall for me

For you, for you are the classic expression of a beautifully formed heart
And I was not expecting it
But you are

The Archangel Sutras

Hallucination of love

I saw your face on every person
You were everywhere
You were all around
How you've haunted me with images from the past
Were you a hallucination[25]?
Or were you really there?
I was never sure
It all seemed so real
Just like dry sand falling through open fingers

So I searched for you
In the faces of strangers walking by
Yet you were no where to be found
Just a lost and lonely boy
That I loved so much

That I love you

Did I scare you with my truth?
That I miss you when you are not around?
That I think of you when you are not there
Hoping to catch you unaware?
In a corridor within a room
I would deceive time to be with you

But I never wanted you to see me like this
I want that picture perfect illusion that's in my head
But without that old sort of dread
That you are in love with someone else

Is my truth to hard to take?
That I love you!
Did I make a mistake?
Or are you forever mine?
And I'll just wait for the right time
But these are things I'll never say

The Archangel Sutras

Just in case I scare you away

I just want something to love
Is that asking too much?
Because I am tired of "things"
I want people

But not as possessions to be locked away
But as something to cherish and set free
And know that they belong to me
Through those invisible bonds
That tie one human to another in what is
otherwise known as love

Gouri Sadotra

The Archangel Sutras

<u>Falling in love</u>

I wanted to fall in love with you
Even before I met you
Or does that mean that I already do?
Tell me, or do you want me to tell you?

For this is a strange unspoken love story
When will you speak to me your unspoken words?
That you wish to whisper unheard
Unheard by everyone other than myself

When all I want you to do is
To shout out loud that you echo my mirror image emotions
That we can match anybody else's love story
And magnify it more than one million times

One more time tell me
Is this what true love sounds like to you?

Gouri Sadotra

Your invisible presence

Where the darkened forces of the universe
clash and collide
United in hatred
They my enemies try to resurrect a sense of
nothingness

But I can always feel your invisible presence
You are always there
I think I love you
Maybe I always have

And if I could command the forces of heaven
and earth against those who are my enemies

I would bid them to stand still
To stand in silence
So that I can once more run forwards
Run towards you and enclose ourselves
Surrounded by a little piece of god's earth

The Archangel Sutras

called home

India
My home
My people
My part of the planet
Where I belong in the final act
When the fire and dust finally settle between
my toes

And throughout this I remember you always
Despite the smiles we have yet to share
And for the teardrops yet to be shed
And for all the kisses yet to be kissed
For I just want to sink into you
For I think
I love you
Have loved you
Will love you
Do love you all over again
Anonymously

Gouri Sadotra

Girls like me

Now you must be very happy
Because you have finally got your revenge
over me
How you must gloat over your revenge
Revenge over girls like me

And you sit there silently smirking
Contemplating your victory
Over my sex
Over my race
And ultimately over and above me

You have left me with nothing
And no one
And now you ask me
Why I am not happy
Did my smile displease you
So much so that you had to destroy it
Obliterating all traces of any positive

emotions from my face

The final one act play has dawned
Where happiness has crystallised into hatred
and contempt

For every time I now see you
My hatred is resurrected
For this now how I imagine you to be

Flickering flame

What did he see in her
That did not could not exist in me?
Why am I always the unhappy one?
Isn't there something or someone made just
for me?

Tell me, which flame flickering did you see
in her
That has been extinguished within me?
That made you love her?
Evermore

Jump start myself

You've stolen the little happiness's
From me as well
And it was the little happiness's that kept me
going
For there are no big happiness's left in my
life

Too much has happened to me
For me to ever be happy here again
All my happiness's have long since left me
And now even my howl is silent

You had to take even my smile away from me
You had to take even the song that I carried in
my heart

For you were ever jealous of my smile
Ever jealous that I could gather the small
happiness's that my life had to offer

The Archangel Sutras

For the big happiness's always seemed to
evade me and elude my grasping heart
As it grasped and gulped
Desperate for some sort of affection or love
But always finding none left for me
Always running on empty
As I jerked and jostled through every heart
beat
Jump starting myself again and again
Once again avoiding the inevitable death that
comes from a broken heart

And a broken heart is a seriously life
threatening condition
And can easily result in sudden death through
suicide
Was that your oblique intention
To shake the very foundations of my life
leaving nothing untainted
nothing pure
and everything contaminated with vice
Wow I realise that it was

Once again back to the beginning looking for
happiness
Once again
Will it ever find me
Or am I a blind man searching aimlessly

Egyptian Eyes

She sat back
Perfectly poised
Perfectly positioned to observe him
Up down and around
With her kohl blackened Egyptian eyes
Ever alert to the world surrounding them
And he looked back with the hooded eyelids of
the sleepy eyed
For it was past midnight

Her once opened hair was a veil of cascading
darkness
Like a wave in motion
From which she half hid her beauty behind
Her characteristic gestures
Every expression of amore
He could only imagine
How she was when she was younger

The Archangel Sutras

Sometimes his own thoughts spoke to her
Through his expressions
And she answered back

As she waited to reply
And then she said
I wanted to enjoy watching your reactions
As realisation of reality slowly set in
That you, that you
Had fallen in love with me

The Archangel Sutras

For I already know

For I already know
She imagines that she loves him
And how he loves her

Him with the dimpled face
And the pleasing pleasant features
And the rough reddish curls
That form a frame all around his head
And finally with the darkened disguised eyes
That soften as and when he speaks
And he speaks

Is there a small safe corner of your heart safe for me?
For I want a reservation of love without reserve

And I tell you once again
Don't ever disappoint my broken heart

The Archangel Sutras

For I wait upon your every word
For I want to be your childhood love
Because the very first taste of love is the
sweetest and the most enduring
And the love that blossoms in the very in the
first flush of youth's innocence
Is the strongest and the purest

And I will wait for an eternity and a day
Until the sands of time runneth over

Mr Butterfly

She met her butterfly today, who visits her
Enchanted garden whilst I am away
His pale yellow gossamer wings that flutter
against the breeze
Tell me Mr Butterfly, how do you hold your
sway against the wind in the trees?

He comes to the garden to visit just like the birds
and the honeybees
To meet the fish in the pond gliding hidden
beneath moss covered leaves
And the pale pink water lilies nestled in waters
deep

To nod to Mrs Frog and her gaggle of tiny tots
Who one day promise to leap past the pond's
platform way up above
That forms a jungle of heart shaped leaves

The Archangel Sutras

Against the bay leaf bush that shivers and shakes
Rustling its leaves both golden and green

Back to the butterfly that flickers and floats far
above lichen[26] encrusted paths
That criss-cross through spongy green lawns
And the amber flowerbeds tucked in between the
cherry trees

So you noticed your butterfly and all his friends
that visit your secret garden
But you never noticed me

Gouri Sadotra

The sweetest smile

Just because you always smile sweetly
And say that I'll never write again
For there is nothing more to say
Whatever was left to be told has already been said
In a million myriad ways
Now you always say that
But then you always think of something to write about
It's never ending with you
Your eternal pout now soothes me
For I know you will find a way
For you have created a world out of words
And will always continue to do so

Mutterings

I want to see the bodily embodiment
Of that soft lilting voice
That whispers his good wishes to me
I hear other people speak on his behalf
Telling me, talking to me
Being my friend
And at that moment
For it is just the merest moment
I am at one with that voice
That voice that whispers his love for me
That imagines a beautiful future for us
As I catch the tale end of mutterings–
Who is he?

The Archangel Sutras

Kiss your face

I am no longer angry with you
For you have defeated me
How I began to hate you
But now all I long to do is to kiss your face time and time again

For there is no time left for anyone else or for anything else
For you have broken my heart a million times
But now I can't bear to be without you
And I will take all those tiny pieces and carry them with me
Don't do it again, I want to tell you
But I know you will
And I know that I will bear it

Because a broken heart is better than no heart at all
Just to feel is to be alive

Gouri Sadotra

The Archangel Sutras

But absence of emotion creates a vacuum
Creates a living corpse
For love, hate, emotion, tears, jealousy, envy
Good and bad are what makes our world come alive
And I can tolerate everything as long as I can be with you
Every moment with you is precious
And I will hold onto it for an eternity

For you
For you are everything to me
And I'll kiss your rosebud coloured lips
And touch your ashen cheeks

When our glances meet again
In that snap shot of time
Where that moment that merest moment
When your eyes talk to me again
And tell me what your mouth cannot

Gouri Sadotra

Fresh faced beauty

For she was a fresh faced and dewy eyed beauty
Both captivating and compelling simultaneously
All locked up in her ivory tower of innocence
That citadel[27] of her mind
That he threatened to destroy
Wholeheartedly

Red raw lips

For your lips are the deepest shade of pink
As if you brought the blood to your lips
By biting into them repeatedly with your small teeth
But no that is just their natural colour
Red raw lips
Yet so delicious to taste
The very colour of ripened pomegranates
For I'd like to bite into your skin with my teeth
And draw some blood
If only to savour that sea of red
And a drop would suffice
If you would be so kind as to oblige
For I want to leave my indelible mark on you
A stamp for the world
To show that you are forever mine
And mine alone

Love at first glance

That was love
For the first time
For I recognised its expression on his face
Through a side wards glance and then it was gone
Only to return in my absence
Was it to catch me unaware?
I don't know
For the mental construction I had in my mind of him vanished
And all that was left was that loving gaze
That I saw from the corner of my eyes
For the merest moment
For that was all it was
Had I blinked I would have missed it

Over and over
I replayed that expression in my head
Whilst trying to analyse an expression of an emotion

The Archangel Sutras

That belonged to someone else
What did it mean?
For me it meant everything
But for him?
What of him
What did he feel?
What did he really feel?
Was that half smile meant for me?
I hoped so

Emotional fatality

You know how I feel about you
Our relationship
This emotional fatality
The numbness that comes with betrayal

Yes betrayal behind those innocent tear streaming eyes
That soft lilting voice
Willing me into submission again and again and again
How you have hypnotised me
Beguiled me with gentle words
And caressed me with softer kisses
For I love to kiss you again and again

And not to touch those poisonous lips that drip with delicious lies
That I can eat so easily
Is an intoxicating pain

The Archangel Sutras

Even as I kiss you
And your poison infuses into my blood
But I want you
And I can't resist

To possess you
To touch you
To feel every inch of you
For I love you
Only you

For this heady concoction of venom and vice
Eternal unending
For I have lived one thousand lives
And died just as many times
In your arms
And I love you still
As I know that you live within me

Gouri Sadotra

Half in love

For I am already half in love with you already
And if I could extinguish that half
My better half
Of that half heart that belongs to you
Then half heartedly I would
For to extinguish that half
Would be to destroy the whole
And that kernel
That living breathing life force
That it contains deep within

Eternity and a day

I'll wait for you for an eternity and a day
Until the very hands of time runneth out
Just as long as I know that you are waiting for me

For this question I ask again and again
To the gatekeepers of the Gods
Until the golden hands of time crack and fail
Against eons of eternities
Against time's eternal boundaries

For this I promise to you
I'll wait for you
Until we meet in the four dimensions of space and time

And we will forever hold hands against eternity's calamities and curses

The Archangel Sutras

And we will create our boundaries
For our love to fill in the spaces

The Archangel Sutras

HORROR POEMS

Mythical creatures

In the age of Elizabeth[28]
Where the devil dreams under the blackest of
blue storms
The inky blue swirling skies are stirring
A veritable melting pot
Awash with shades of blue
Merging into one living breathing thunderstorm,
High up in the heavens
A physical manifestation expressing the anger of
the Gods

And I am chasing imaginary Chinese dragons
Through the portals of my mind
And into the labyrinth I fall

This is a labyrinth[29] where you are the Minotaur[30]

And I am dragged closer into the serpent's lair

The Archangel Sutras

As you watch me twist and turn
Like coils of curls on Medusa's[31] crown
Your hair itself is a serpent's snare deep within
your lair

And the only rule
Is that once you comprehend what the rules are
The rules change and a new and more dangerous
game begins
With a permanent and tireless opponent that
never sleeps

For the rules denature and die
And then reform
Into a new and more credible mythical creature of
the mind

Once you comprehend the incomprehensible
Then the rules change
But the game
That eternal game continues unabated
Fighting an increasingly tireless opponent that

The Archangel Sutras

never sleeps

And now you are a silent enemy
You utter only noiseless threats
That no one else can decipher
But still the danger never ends
And always against a backdrop of death
My certain death
As you wait for me to fall into a trap of my own making

For this un-eerie silence is deafening
As I cry my noiseless scream.
A noiseless death
Followed by a silent scream
By an invisible enemy
That is nameless and shapeless
But can take any form

Like a king cobra waiting for the right time to pounce

Gouri Sadotra

The Archangel Sutras

You the multi-headed living breathing mythical
beast that roars

You watch me through the eye
Of the all seeing
All knowing
And ever present Cyclops[32]
And I wait and watch your hatred unfold in front
of me

This is not the end
But the beginning
Because I cannot convert you
Or convince you
I can only kill you with kindness

Tell me
How do I escape from Midnight's garden?
From which no soul has ever escaped
Unharmed unarmed and alive?

And I realise that we are all as fragile as china

dolls
Trapped beneath the stirring skies of a
thunderstorm

Hellhounds[33]

My soul escapes from myself
When being me is too much to bear
So I no longer have to hear the taunts of the
entire world
Which beckons me to end it all
End my life
The end
Death

When there is no reason left to live
And no one left to love
When even hope has abandoned me
When my heart feels restless and aloof
It tells me that it feels such terrible pain
A stabbing pain
A constant ache

It asks me how to end it?
And I don't know what to say

The Archangel Sutras

When all I want to do is die right away
Only then
Only then will the hellhounds that pursue me
Through my thoughts
Go away

But in my restless hours I know no peace
I know that that pack of hellhounds that pursue me
Through the dark meandering alleyways of my mind
Aim to tear me to shreds
They won't rest until every last fragment of me
My own originality is destroyed
The hellhounds that pursue me through the channels of my mind
I want to end it all
And say adios forever

The pack of hellhounds that pursue me even
Through the twilight hours
They won't even let me escape from myself

The Archangel Sutras

Even in my half-life they goad me to relinquish
the rest of me
To part company piece by piece
And I am in physical pain and mental anguish
There is not a part of me that has not been hurt

Even when they burn me alive
With their words and gestures and half truths
I say to myself
One day I will pull myself together
Form a new whole
A new completeness
An upgraded version of me
A better brighter being

But every second I struggle with myself
I watch and I wait
As I hear the realities of my life become warped
and denatured
As they tumble from the growling, salivating,
drooling, gnashing jaws
Of the hell hounds

Gouri Sadotra

The Archangel Sutras

Those hellhounds that pursue me through the
dark recesses of my mind
Every waking hour and every second that I try to
sleep

Self perpetuating hatred

Don't ever make the mistake of feeling sorry for them
For having any sympathy
For if you do they will crush you
And your sympathy
By using your weakness for there so called plight
Against you
Another opportunity to manipulate you
And make you bend to their collective will

To see you emotionally and intellectually disheveled[34]
And ultimately destroyed
Because in order for them to survive
You have to be proved wrong again and again
And they are able and willing to make your life a barren and desolate wilderness
With neither friends nor family
With no support

The Archangel Sutras

To isolate you
From everyone and everything

To make you forget that even the smallest
kindness ever existed
To make you forget yourself
In this self perpetuating hatred
And ultimately destroy your own life
Leaving death as the only corridor
The only exit which you will come to greet
willingly
And wait for with increasing despair
As they shout out the voices
Of those guardian angels that seek to guide you
That offer hope
And a way out of this conundrum of allegations
That they can't quite reach you
But are always invisibly there
That screams through the voices of those
shadows

Gouri Sadotra

The Archangel Sutras

That surrounds you when you think that you are most alone

Of taking tablets

My hatred of you has gotten the better of me
So I take tablets to control my temperament
To make me sweetly spoken and compliant
To cool the fire that rages in my brain
And finally to dispel the notion that I ever
disliked you

Minds' eye[35]

When I am most afraid and mostly alone
You come to visit me
Haunting me with your magical illusions
And I am locked in a permanent battle of wills
with you
All acted out on a mental plane
And you come to me in many guises and
disguises
To taunt me, to torment me
To offer false hope
And you watch me and wait for me
Willing me to fail
How I want to be able to wish you away
But you are always there
Within my mind's eye
Both hateful and heartless
Waiting for the right moment
Ever ready to spring into action
At the notice of the merest moment

The Archangel Sutras

Invisible you

I don't know who, invisible you
Don't talk to me
Don't touch me
Although I know that you want to
Because you have frightened me to death

You are insidious
You are infectious
You are all around
Who are you?
Invisible you
Will I ever know your name?

Are you trying to scare me?
Or are you trying to warn me?
Or is it a bit of both?
What is your true motive?
I don't know

The Archangel Sutras

You've silenced me
Shut my mouth
So I cannot speak the truth
Because if I did who would believe me
Because you have not shown to them
What you've shown to me
They will doubt me
They will smile sweetly
And say that I am slowly going mad
So I stay quiet
Just watching and waiting
For the next act to unfold
Before my eyes
For the next truth to be revealed
Before my eyes
And my eyes alone

The Archangel Sutras

The voices from outside

Not even we can protect you
If you go outside
Said the voices from outside
Your house is protected
By an invisible fortress
Resurrected from above
From which no enemy
Outside or otherwise
Can enter without permission

However the invisible daemons[36]
Howl at you with their half lies
And half lives
As you walk through
As you walk through
The dusty draughty corridors of your house

I ignore them all
You can blow them all away
If you know how

Gouri Sadotra

The Archangel Sutras

For you have the know how
And know how to use it

For they are the shadows that stalk you
Sometimes tempting you
Other times taunting you
And torturing you
And finally telling you
To do things that you would not otherwise do
Goading you to go outside to face the danger
That they say exists only in your mind

And the voices from outside grow more vocal
and vociferous
Sometimes sweet
Sometimes shrilled
And finally screaming
Beckon you to come outside with their sweet
whys
Why don't you meet us?
Why don't you like us?
Why don't you come outside

Gouri Sadotra

The Archangel Sutras

As they chant you name again and again
As if it is a curse to be resurrected

Stone wall

Why do you think I'm a stone wall?
You see no reflection of emotion in my eyes
But you have to look closer
To see how my eyes darken from person to person's gaze
How I blink quickly
How my eyebrows arch

If you looked behind the veil
You would see how much pain I am in
How I see everything
Feel everything
Understand everything
And I don't want to hurt you with my depth of feeling
With the pain I carry
So I barricade my feelings in
Can you take the intensity of my glaze?

The Archangel Sutras

I don't want to see you turn away in horror
To see your knuckles turn white as you gasp for breathe
A Real life freakshow in slow motion

I feel it, because I see it
And it hurts to watch you fall
To see your pain
And it hurts me to be like this
But I cannot change

I don't want your sympathy, your pity
I appreciate your concern, I really do
But it's your understanding that I really want
But is it possible to understand without feeling?
And is it possible to understand me without feeling what I feel?
At the intensity that I feel it?

What I wouldn't give to be you!
To feel that lukewarm emotion

The Archangel Sutras

You tell me "Stonewall wear your heart on your sleeve"
"Because I want to see and feel that emotional interaction"
But when you feel it, you turn away
My suffering is too much for you to bear
Can you stand it – to see it
So how can you bear it – to hear it
So I lay, stonewalled into submission

The Archangel Sutras

Waiting for Angels

The demons don't ever meet them
Don't let them go near you
They will try to trick you
And tease you

And in this manner extract all the secrets to your
defences
For it is true that they want to know your secrets
The secrets of the angels that you guard
That you summon to help you

And how time and time again you evade and defy
them
With your magic
Without them ever finding out how or where or
When these angels are and
Where they reside

The Archangel Sutras

How they speak in unison to defy my enemies
again and again
And defend me in mortal combat
In this invisible battle of wills
Which is being fought in the skies?
In the soaring heavens above

How my enemies tell lies
And pretend that the angels are no longer on my side
As they try to confuse me thereby tricking me into doing something wrong
For they have written the rules of this game of which I know nothing about
That I am learning through trial by fire

For my enemies want to meet me
And decant the secrets of my soul
Through their trickery and lies
But I will wait for the angels
I always wait for the angels

Gouri Sadotra

The Archangel Sutras

That they try to silence through pursed lips
And I wait for the friendly voices of the angels
That speak no lies
So I wait and watch and wait again for the angels
That dare to speak through the mouths of my enemies
Echoing their threats to all my other enemies around

Weakness

If you are ever given a choice
Pick a weak body over a weak mind
Because psychological damage through warfare
Can be more insidious than physical force

Once you destroy the mind
You destroy the person
Once you destroy the body
The body dies but the name lives forever
They are martyrs
And their names live on through their deeds
Good bad or other wise

Beware beautiful child

So know beautiful child
What he is capable of
Even though he has not done it to you
Just yet
For your time will come
If you are not wary
If you are not wise
So remember that we can be trapped by our own limitations
That our weaknesses that we thought that we hide so well
Burn like beacons in a cloudless night sky
Attracting all that want to harm us
And use us
That want to
And are willing
To use our weaknesses against us
For remember beautiful child
It takes intelligence not to be used

The Archangel Sutras

Especially time and time again

Gnarled beauty

I wish to hide from the world
You don't know how ugly and gnarled[37] I am on
the inside
And still you call me beautiful
To my snarling contemptuous self
You've only seen my veneer
Because that is all I have permitted you to see
Please don't come any closer
Point your radar away from me
As your penetrating glare exposes my inner core
My hateful self that I loathe
And wish to hide from the world

Citadel of the mind

For it was the citadel of the mind
That needed to be overcome
After that everything would become easy
And she would come to him herself
Willingly
And he would destroy her previously held
Pre-conceptions
Brick by brick

Corrupting power

You may call it a moral victory to survive
Call it what you may
But always remember the corrupting influence of power
How it may affect undecided victims
Those that flicker with indecision against their conscience
At the thought of that temporary financial gain
That is merely the bait that draws them in
Time and time again

Othello and Macbeth

Human nature is filled with deceit
For there are no absolutes in life
And every characteristic flawed
Some love too much
Like Othello[38]
Others love too little
Like Macbeth[39]

And sometimes people do the strangest things
seemingly out of character
As if reacting against their own nature
That was part of the dynamics of any relationship
with him
He tried to create conflict in order to get the
worst out of you
And put you through a series of non-stop tests
To find out who you truly are
And what you are capable of

The Archangel Sutras

And the ebb and flow of provocation was incessant
As he drew you to reveal all the shades of your shadow
On a merry go round of his making
Yes he was a master manipulator
And that was his invention
Because he truly enjoyed it
Always testing always trying
Because he believed the possibility of anything

The Archangel Sutras

<u>Adultery</u>

Old age, it happened to us
But adultery did not have to
You the perpetrator
And me the silent witness

For I want to hear about a word in particular
"Infidelity"
Such a deliciously delicate sounding word
That dances on the lips

No explanations
No embellishments[40]
Nothing, just the unadulterated truth
From your deceitful lips
And lying tongue

Tell me now
Tell me the truth
Do you have any confessions to make to me?

Gouri Sadotra

The Archangel Sutras

Any apologies to admit
Any corrections to carry through?

I have already heard a list of lies

Tasting of teardrops as I speak
In the shadow of your tears you weep

Where did you find those beauties?
Behind bars?
The rag doll expression in their eyes
Their jagged appearance
With their dull vacant eyes
Yearning, nay pleading
For the childhood that they never had
With the rosebud not yet faded from their sunken cheeks

Plea-bargaining
Trusting no one
As much the victim and the vixen

Gouri Sadotra

The Archangel Sutras

And you
Your once raven rich hair
Now turned old and ashen
And your golden skin a shade of mottled grey
As you fight for your final flights of fancy

An adulterated adulterer
You didn't become perfect in one day
You became perfect by practice

How many times did you find the beauties beneath?
For I have imagined you many times in my mind
Who are these women escaping towards you?
I want to know
And I want to know now!

Captive in your eyes

People ask me with their eyes
"Tell me, what is it like to have all of those
people staring at you all of the time?"
"What is it like to be talked about and told lies?"
Then I look at them and reply

"Your thoughts are no secret to me"
"Do you really imagine that I don't know what
you think of me and why?"
"For I can feel your glances on my body
Like one hundred pairs of invisible hands
touching me from afar"
"For I know now how you think about me from
your most minute expressions
That pulsates outwards towards me
Like the indestructible radioactivity emitted from
an atom bomb

There I lay captured through an all-seeing

The Archangel Sutras

kaleidoscopic[41] web of eyes
Consisting of men, women and children

Is anyone exempt from this grazing gaze?
No one, only I

Self destruction

Don't keep any hatred alive in your heart
For that is the wound that festers and grows
Until all that is left is to self-destruct

Like the suicide victim
That harms not only himself
But also destroys all those around him
In a massive act of self-harm
For a cause common to no one
For this is a huge act of hatred
Of the common purpose of humanity

Of bruises

These purple blue-black bruises
On my off white skin
Hardly picturesque
So I cover up with western clothes
From head to toe
Albeit dressed in western clothes
With the intention that these purple blue black bruises
Stamped with your fist
On my off white body
Covered to hide our tug of love-hate
Our push pull secret
Ever sealed with your kiss

Alice in Wonderland[42]

I'm not Alice and this isn't Wonderland
This is the nightmare that never ends
And I am trapped on all sides with my enemies
surrounding me
As they lay siege to the citadel that is my house
Waiting for the right time to kill
And as I wait
I'm not getting bigger
But this house is getting smaller
Rather like inverse Alice in Wonderland
Exactly in reverse
"Eat me"
"Drink me"
And I do
But I don't get any bigger
Only this house
Gets smaller and smaller

The Archangel Sutras

Let the devil decide the details

I cannot bear to see her suffer
To see her slowly go mad
To see her slowly robbed of her sanity
Letting the very source of insanity reveal
itself in full flow

So I'll kill her
As softly as snowflakes and just as melting

As they plot my destruction
As they plot my downfall
As they plan my demise

And you can take me dark angel
To where I truly belong
To either heaven or hell
Or maybe to the netherworld
And back
where no soul belongs

Gouri Sadotra

The Archangel Sutras

And I will let you decide
I'll let you cast my deeds both good and bad
Like a pair of dice
And let the devil decide the details
I'll let the devil choose where I should live
Long after I die

And I will try to be nice to everyone
To make my last moments as peaceful and
painless as can be
Whilst I prepare to die
As time is my witness
And reason is my hostage
So be kind
Be quick
Because all real hope has abandoned me

Kill

It's either kill or be killed
But as I have no intention of dying at this
moment
I guess it's still your turn

For every step I take towards my safety
You take one step closer towards death
Even sudden death

Suddenly I've realised that the longevity of my
life
Depends on your collective imminent deaths
So you will have to die for me to live

Your heart's desire

Firstly I will find out what your heart truly
desires most of all
Then I will ensure that you never, never
possess it ever
With all the powers I possess
Not until my last dying breath escapes my lips

A prayer from the dying

Throughout the ages there have always been
warrior priests[43]
Priests that do battle with the forces of evil
In whatever form or manifestation they may take
So I call them
Spirits of the ages
The eternal guardians of righteous consciousness

Let you rise from the depths of your watery
graves
Because I call to you in my hour of need
To rise up and protect me against the evil
That the darkness brings forth

For I am a warrior princess[44]
And I call to you spirits to protect me in my
dying hour
To protect my soul

The Archangel Sutras

Because they attack me metaphysically
Through the citadel of my mind
So make me strong
To deflect all those arrows laced with hatred
That threatens to poison me
Make my mind so strong
So in my dying moments I feel only peace
So I may die a glorious death
On the battlefield of life
And not the half-life of a coward
Filled with regrets

Make me immortal in death as in life
As I lay down my arms
I whisper a prayer
A prayer from the dying
Pray for me until no remaining embers of me
burn alive[45]

Gouri Sadotra

The Archangel Sutras

MISCELLANEOUS POEMS

Talking to the spirits of the ages

I wanted to raise the spirits of the dead from their
graves
Sophocles[46], Socrates[47], Byron[48], Wilde[49]
I called to you to come to me

Tell me about your life, tell me about your life
because books are not enough
And so I charted my imagination
And I called to you
And you traveled through space and time to meet
me

To see you because I always did know how to
travel through time
As I sat on the corner of the mountain top with
my face towards the sunset standing with my
hands out
With your captured prose on paper

Gouri Sadotra

The Archangel Sutras

I inhaled the sights of you
the sounds of you
the smell of you

A professor once asked me
Do you want to create something for the future?
And as I always said
Yes, to stand the test of eternity

I always did know how to travel through space
and time
To branch the gap between the past and the future
To create immortality

A professor once asked me
Do you want to be famous?
Because I thought you wanted to be good?
To be great
And I told him
That is all I ever hoped to achieve
That's all I ever wanted

Gouri Sadotra

The Archangel Sutras

I told my professor
I never wanted fame if it was based on the
premise that I was pretending to be something
that wasn't real

I only ever really wanted to be good
Because in the final analysis
I knew that stood the test of time
And that's how I know how to travel through
time

How to be immortal, through the greatness of
your work
Elvis[50] knew it
Socrates knew it
Even Van Gogh[51] knew it

The secret of time travel
How to travel to the future
How to talk to the future and share your voice
Because as Decartes[52] pointed out to me
When you read, you are having a conversation

Gouri Sadotra

The Archangel Sutras

with me

By a turn of the page
You resurrect them from the dead
You breathe life into them
Through their works
Make them immortal
Make me immortal

Shakespeare traveled through time
Bacon[53], Marlowe[54], Keats[55] et cetera
This is the only true test of immortality that we know

The Archangel Sutras

<u>The little mermaid</u>[56]

Just like the little mermaid
Who sold her voice
For the gift of a pair of feet
That dance like a pair of white doves
I lost my voice
And every word I try to speak
Makes me bleed from the inside

Just like the little mermaid
Who sold her voice
For the gift of dance
I am no longer able to speak
The way I once did

So speaking to the heavens
Through my minds' eye
I beg of you
Release my voice
And summon the forces of the heavens

Gouri Sadotra

The Archangel Sutras

To protect me here on earth

Make me whole
Make me complete once more
Reunite me with myself
So that my voice can soar into the heavens
And fly once again

Your approval

Your approval! Hah I sneer at it
Your approval?
Who are you to approve of me?
Say that this action was right?
Say that this action was wrong?
Judge me on my merits
Or on my merest movements
To try to control me with your disapproval

What gives you the right to judge me?
What do you know that is so great?
So amazing, so profound?

Are you a philosopher?
Are you a psychiatrist?
Are you God?
That your every word has weight?
That your every word has gravitas?

The Archangel Sutras

I despise your sycophantic[57] zeal!
Your obsession with me
You judge me on my merits
And then you award demerits

Who are you?
Are you the Lord High Executioner?
To tie a noose around my neck?
To order my execution?
For my high crimes and misdemeanours
For my high treason and high crimes

For my so called crimes against humanity?
I despise you and everything you represent

You who has no original thought
You who has no original word
You who doesn't dream your own dreams
Or live your own life

You who relies on everyone else to tell you who your opinion is

Gouri Sadotra

The Archangel Sutras

You are the ultimate second hander

You see nothing
You hear nothing
You feel nothing

Unless you are told, look, listen, feel, hear.

I liked you better when you hated me
I respected you more when you found me
When I proclaimed my genius – you laughed

How dare I?
Who am I to decide?
Who am I to forge my own destiny?
Who am I to live my own life

You talk to me now because you think that I may have celebrity
So that I may be a cause celebre[58]

Gouri Sadotra

The Archangel Sutras

You push me down
So I grow wings
I try to fly and you shoot me down

How does it harm you that I want to be a comet?
That I want to soar above the Milky Way and glow?

I perceive you
I unwrap you
I reveal you
Your dark nature
Your dark side

Be ordinary
Be average
Be like everyone else
Be like us you say

And I've tried God knows
I've tried
But I cannot be what you want me to be

Gouri Sadotra

The Archangel Sutras

Between purity and hygiene

In humble obedience to the Gods and
Goddesses of the Hindu pantheon[59]
Let me explain the difference between purity
and hygiene in food

Food can be pure without being hygienic
Or food can be hygienic without being pure

To be made pure is to use unadulterated fresh
ingredients and giving offerings to God
Whilst hygienic food can quite simply be
adulterated or not
It simply implies that it is bacteria free, virus
free, and infection free
But no offering has been made to God
Or even the ingredients involved may or may
not be suitable to give as an offering to God[60]

Purity also implies all forms of religious
ritual cleansing has been perpetrated on the

person the implements and the offerings
Whereas cleanliness simply means to make clean

Shakespeare's sister[61]

Against the backdrop
Against the stench of immortality
If I, if I, in slavish imitation of Shakespeare
If I am Shakespeare
Then she then she is by all accounts
Christopher Marlowe

After all who was a contemporaneous[62] figure
to Shakespeare in real time and geographical
location
Who was falsely attributed to writing
Shakespeare's works

And finally who was considered to be a lesser
orb to Shakespeare on the literary landscape
For she, for she was Shakespeare's sister

Self realisation

Self realisation is better than being told
Because you do not abdicate analysis
Of any given situation
And you know the reasons why any such
action or actions
Are taken against you

You have a firm foundation
On which to seat the truth
Whilst your enemies try to unseat you

Because many times knowing the answer is
not enough
You need to be able to analyse
This way you can defend yourself against any
of the myriad multi-pronged attacks
Against yourself
So learn the truth
But also learn the reasons behind it

For there is not such thing as absolutes
When we talk about concepts like
Self realisation

A lot of it depends on human perception and opinion
Which are malleable concepts at bet
And in there lies the greater truth in its entire spectrum

Childhood friends

Whilst I cannot extrapolate[63] the value of
My blossoming "half-love" backwards in
time

I do wish that we had been
Hand in hand
Holding hands
The best of childhood friends
Growing up together
Growing old together

For I want to be your friend first and foremost
And for you to always feel that I am worthy of
that friendship

For I already know
She imagines that she loves him
And how he loves her

The Archangel Sutras

Him with the dimpled face
And the pleasing pleasant features
And the rough reddish curls
That form a frame all around his head
And finally with the darkened disguised eyes
That soften as and when he speaks
And he speaks

Is there a small safe corner of your heart safe for me?
For I want a reservation of love without reserve

And I tell you once again
Don't ever disappoint my broken heart
For I wait upon your every word
For I want to be your childhood love
Because the very first taste of love is the sweetest and the most enduring
And the love that blossoms in the very in the first flush of youth's innocence

Gouri Sadotra

The Archangel Sutras

Is the strongest and the purest

And I will wait for an eternity and a day
Until the sands of time runneth over

Of children

Children that are taught to lie
Taught to cheat
Taught to steal
Taught to hate
That are treated with cruelty with anger
They are not like that to begin with

You will find that a child untainted is the
biggest advocate of truth and justice
For children are borne pure
But in society's environment
Family
Friends
Twists and turns
That child denatures
And their very nature that was once
Innocent and good
Changes to make them full of hateful
thoughts and harbingers of wicked deeds

The Archangel Sutras

Children are the future
But that future needs to be molded and
shaped with
Intelligence
And love and patience

The very second a child is born
Society's pressures are imposed upon them
With greater force than the earth's very
atmosphere

If you want to destroy a person's personality
You need to destroy the child within
For every hurt inflicted leaves invisible
scratches on the brain's memory
And repeated assaults on the brain
Scars that person's behaviour, actions and
thoughts
In fact every aspects of their very being

How adults destroy

The Archangel Sutras

The very children that they set out to improve
and educate
By repeatedly inflicting their own prejudices
And inferiority complexes on those very
children

Adults are comparable to clay baked in a
pottery kiln
Impossible to mold and easy to break
Where as children are the very grains of earth
That can form any feature again and again
Form and reform
Molded and remolded
Fashioned and refashioned
Again and again
To create and recreate new and greater
entities

To mold an adult's mind
Once their personality is fully formed
Once their nature is formed
Is near impossible

Gouri Sadotra

The Archangel Sutras

And to change a person from within you need to challenge them
When they were a child

The Archangel Sutras

<u>Chess pieces</u>

His greatest strength
Lay in the fact
That both enemies and friends alike
Underestimated his intentions

Hence any challenge
To his intelligence or abilities
Was always somewhat under prepared

In the sloppy half hearted manner
Of an over-confident cockerel[64]
That crows his own forthcoming victory
From morning to dusk
Before the game is won
Whilst he stealthily maneuvered
The people around him as if
They were chess pieces on a chessboard

On books

For books are the very best of companions
As the writer has distilled their very essence
Of the very best of what they are and what they know
Put it into a book and published it

The Archangel Sutras

Lawyers

Do you understand the meaning behind this magic?
He who understands the meaning of all shades of magic
Who else but a lawyer
The ultimate wordsmith
Who understands the true meaning behind words?
And how to twist them to serve his or her own purposes
To turn your days into nights and your nights into a non-stop hell
So that you doubt the veracity[65] behind your own sanity

So don't doubt the veracity behind your own sanity
And don't waste your precious words
On the worthless and the unworthy
Remember that same words can be

The Archangel Sutras

Both a sword and a shield in the right hands

Do his words disarm you?
Do his words deceive you?
And finally do his words destroy you?
As you wait and watch with hypnotic fascination
As he sets your whole world alight with his words

Sun and Moon

All he wears is his crown of golden hair down to
the ground
All watch his naked feet dance
Like a pair of turtledoves in love in the long grass
While he serenades the summer with sounds to
all around

"Ah to be king of the heavens and lord of the
skies for just one day"
The west wind whispers as he whistles by

And the sun and the moon exchange glances
While they exchange places
As they make their move across the heavens
Beyond and below

And then as twilight dawns
The sun glides past the earth to say goodnight
And plant a kiss high up in the heavens

Gouri Sadotra

The Archangel Sutras

Where the sun and moon almost collide

And then the moon salutes the sun
As she makes her ascent upon the skies
While the sun disappears down behind the horizon.

And we are left alone
Bathed in the silvery blue light of a lesser moon
Which gazes no less bewitchingly
With its silvery stare to all and beyond
Beckoning young lovers to once again dance in the moonlight
And fall in love with each other once again

Gouri Sadotra

The Archangel Sutras

<u>Friends</u>

I wore your dress
Your favourite dress
All starry eyed pretending to be you
For I liked this dress immensely
It was meant to be worn by the Princess of the
Fairies no less
But somehow it came into my hands

I just wanted to own a part of you
In order to be a part of you
So I brought the dress
That dress
Your dress
To tread in your footsteps
And dance in the warm summer rains
So I bought that dress
Only because I knew that you wanted it
And I wanted to be you just for a while

Gouri Sadotra

The Archangel Sutras

To steal your soul
Tame it
And make it my own for a while
Just for a while

Now I don't mind if we don't meet for a while
Because I now know that we are already the best
of friends
And will always be the best of friends
But you already knew that
You were just waiting for me to find out
In my own way

Because I like you best
When you are dancing in the air
Pretending to be a butterfly
And I wanted to be your friend
And we were the best of friends
Even before we met
Weren't we?

Gouri Sadotra

The Archangel Sutras

Childhood memories

A temper always tempered by reason
For he was never really angry it was more play anger
More of a bluff to make you realise your mistake
To make you realise that you were in the wrong
Never to put you down but rather to pull you up

To bring forth an admission of truth from the guilty party
Namely you
And then to surrender a smile sweetly
And accept your apology and the argument is all over

For he was always quick to anger
But never in retaliation or recrimination
Then friends once again
And so the cycle of life continued without hesitation

Gouri Sadotra

The Archangel Sutras

Never to be made to feel that you are unwanted
and unloved
Because of your gender

Never to be repeatedly told that you are a burden
Not even made to feel that way ever

Never made to feel that you are incompetent and
incapable
Of even the simplest thought

To know very truly that there is someone
somewhere
In a long forgotten corner of the world
That loves you very much and thinks of you
repeatedly

In a place that is no longer spoken of not even in
hesitation
At a long forgotten house that even the hands of
time forgot

Gouri Sadotra

The Archangel Sutras

Where you were always loved no matter what you did wrong

To know that your faded childhood photos are still there
Where the dust settles
And sit in their house waiting to greet you when you next walk in

To know that even the frame that holds your photo
Was lovingly picked just for you

To know that there was always room in that house for one more
And no matter how small the rooms were they were always big enough

To know that you were never disbelieved
Not even as a girl child
And this matters
It really matters

Gouri Sadotra

The Archangel Sutras

Or have you forgotten how it feels to be a child

To know that your words carried as much weight
as that of an adult
To know that your every birthday was celebrated
twice
Even when you were not there

But you were always there weren't you
Because memories of you linger on where you
used to play

Did you surrender a little piece of yourself?
When you left for them to keep safe in their
hearts in order to remember you by?

Birds

Observe the heavens
And you will see them gliding by
A silhouette in the sky
They simply open their wings and they fly
Magical musical mammals,
Trained tamed and wild
How I wish that they would eat by my side
Nestling amidst the flora and fauna
What a beautiful sight

A summer's day

Way below in a stream somewhere
Flights of fishes offer flying kisses to the water
nymphs[66]
As they eat their food in the cool waters beneath
and below

In pools teeming with water skaters
Insects punt past on the waters above
Under the summers sun
While trying to catch out the red and black
spotted lady birds
That fly past
As the bumble bees drone by
Gathering nectar from wild flowers
All under this idyllic summer sun

"Don't' give them too much importance"
Bubble the waters to the garden fishes,
As the waters gurgle in their gatherings

The Archangel Sutras

Meandering their way past rocks and pebbles

"What's your hurry?"
Asks the water vole to the silver stream
As the water vole dives into the rushing stream
From the divided long grasses that grow by the riverbanks

"I am rushing out to meet the flying fishes
And the dolphins in waters deep far far away"
Says the silver stream

"You will never get there!"
Croon the water gods to the fresh waters
"You will be diverted!"
As they strum their lyres
And whistle lazily under this idyllic summer's sun

And the water nymphs giggle and gasp
At the presumptuous waters
As they idly fan themselves with the fallen leaves

Gouri Sadotra

The Archangel Sutras

While waiting for the breeze to gather

These water maidens in white dresses
Run their fingers dreamily through the stream
And later gather daisies and other wild flowers
To make crowns of flowers to wear in their
flowing hair

And all this happens under a soft summer's sun
That hangs low in the azure skies
As the day draws to a close

Where is this hazy dreamy place that you speak of?
It lays hidden in my imagination!

The Archangel Sutras

Love of humanity

It's my love of humanity
My love of human beings that keeps me alive
Once you destroy that
You destroy me
Because there is nothing else to live for

For this is what I write about
And whom I write for
So if you ever want to stop me in my tracks
Then simply destroy the basic belief
I have in the goodness of mankind
And then I am finished
Because there is nothing and no one left to dream
for

Where there is evil
There is also good
So let not the evil blind you
To what good there may be lurking within a

The Archangel Sutras

man's spirit
For we are both
Both good and evil intertwined
United until death parts the forces of good and evil
And they go their separate ways

Even though in life they exist for one another
As if they are like the parting waves
That emerge and arise from the ocean bed
They are brothers in arms

So I always have to hope for the best
Even if the worst has to happen
Because once you stop hoping and wishing and spinning dreams out loud
Then the fragrant bloom of life
Lies half dead in your arms and you are finished

Intelligence verses education

A person may lack education
But that does not mean that they lack intelligence

For intelligence is a renewable and indestructible resource
And is ever present
And it is just as bright and shining like the midday sun

Intelligence and education united and in motion
Is a fascinating spectacle to behold
For education can be acquired but intelligence cannot

Education is a hard won commodity
An incremental[67] unit to be wrestled[68] over
That can be bought and sold
But using your intelligence costs nothing

The Archangel Sutras

Education can be forgotten but intelligence
cannot
And once fully developed is an ever present
constant

Education is infinite and unending
Rather like the universe expanding exponentially
Whilst intelligence is always subject to
limitations
To the law of limiting factors

To truly savour your education and intelligence
You need to experience ignorance
Because both are subject to internal and external
pressures
For you cannot destroy intelligence but you can
denature it
And turn something beautiful into a grotesque
caricature of itself
A monster rather like the unspun intelligence of
Dr Jekyll[69]
Who mutated into Mr Hyde[70]

Gouri Sadotra

A young plant

Imagine that a young person is like a plant
It needs all manner of the earth's
And the atmosphere's raw elements
Beaming down on it
In order to grow to its full strength
And to maximise its capabilities
To the level of its full potential
To extrinsically[71] and intrinsically[72]
Nurture all aspects of its development
And then grow

Frenemies[73]

I got used to you

You got used to me

Or maybe we have moved one notch closer to

each other

From enemy to frenemy

But still more enemy that friend

Your move!

Princelings

So I pretended to be a princeling
A prince in hiding
A prince in disguise
And I pretended out loud
With all my other princeling friends
Did anyone recognise me?
Only other princelings
For my robes were as invisible as the emperors new clothes
Tell me, how does it hurt your self esteem that I pretended out loud
That I wanted to be a prince amongst men?

Food

Food is honour, food is love, food is respect
Feeding someone is the equivalent to giving them respect

You can tell how much or how little a person respects or loves you
By not only the volume of food offered
But by its intrinsic value
Both financially and nutritionally
But where issues of nutrition come into play
A person's knowledge, beliefs and value systems are also important

Traditionally, in times of famine it is sign of prosperity to be big in size
But in times of plenty it is a sign of prosperity to be small.

Attitudes towards food and a person's relative

The Archangel Sutras

"fatness" are interlinked
And are inversely proportional to each other
But interestingly it is also linked to their position in society

But in modern times
Wealth is inversely proportional to the waistline
For wealth is not simply measured by the size of a person's waistline
But by the quality, variety and freshness of the type of food that they eat
As we all become increasingly homogeneous and heterogeneous in our choice and tastes in food

Your attitude towards food is the biggest fashion statement of them all
Because public consumption of food is a big fashion faux pas[74]
But abstinence is not allowed either

Imagination

Is imagination such a terrible thing?
For in my imagination I gather snowdrops
And dance in the starlight with fairies
I ride bareback on cream coloured seahorses
On a whisper of a wave that grows and grows

Imagination is the companion I have to entertain and amuse
In your opinion I may be a sickly and lonely child
But in my mind I am the master of the entire universe
A wizard
A wunderkind[75]
In possession of powers that defy description

I can be anyone at anytime and any place
I can placate the gods
Do damage to daemons
Destroy and rebuild all in the wink of an eye

The Archangel Sutras

Whilst being at one with the world
And in harmony with the natural rhythm and
rhyme of life

Imagination is a vast, limitless and wonderful
possession
With it, I can construct citadels in the skies
And with every step that I take
I waltz[76] into a magical world of one
Where all obey my every whim
No matter how wishful or whimsical

Gouri Sadotra

Wondrous child

Wondrous child
Are you somewhere in the heavens?
Maybe dancing from cloud to cloud
Clutching your jetty curls
Still tinkering with your toys
For I am looking forward to meeting you
I am looking forward to greeting you
With outstretched arms

Wondrous child
I know who you are
I know where you are
And I am waiting to take you into my arms and kiss you

Wondrous child
When you are finally born
I am expecting choirs of archangels to sing
That the heavens will weep at loosing you

The Archangel Sutras

And that God himself will answer back

Wondrous child
It is my secret sorrow
That I have not met you yet
My unborn child
I want you to know
That I've already fallen in love with you

The whole world is waiting to tell you
That it is miracle of creation to be borne alive
And live in freedom

Gouri Sadotra

India of my childhood

There is a place
A happy place far, far, away
A place called home
A second home
Where once the magic begins
It never ends
Where people appear without being there
Where sticks and stones turn to dust and ash

Where cobras are there only to disappear
To find that they are shooed away by snake charmers
Residing at every corner of every street

And fairy lights turn on without a switch
But with the double click of your fingertips
And sliding doors open with verbal commands

Where water taps run like river beds

The Archangel Sutras

During the monsoon[77]
Where dust clings to every piece of clothing you wear
But you don't care
Because you can still walk barefoot
Finding God's own earth between your toes

Where horns and bells trill everywhere
And music wafts from every open window

Where silks and satins drape the streets
And every piece of cloth or clothing sold
Has a contrast or a clash of colours

Where vendors sell exotic sweets
And savoury treats
And the fragrant perfume of spices drown the meandering alleyways
And back roads of every gulley[78]

Where there is a festival celebrated with food
every single day of the week

Gouri Sadotra

The Archangel Sutras

Where a pantheon of gods and goddesses still reign
Over the hearts of legions of people
By fulfilling secret wishes and silent prayers
And Yogis[79] and priests bid you into their silent retreat
With a pot pourri of perfumes for sale
Incense leaving its cloudy trail

Where princes dresses like paupers
Mingle in the hot dust stony streets
And every pauper is a prince in disguise in this magical kingdom
And every other person is a poet in the making

Walking through bazaars that are dressed in darkness
With crowds of people still pushing and shoving
As they charm their way through every corner of the markets
It's the Arabian nights[80] all over again

The Archangel Sutras

And the sun sits high in the sky
Like a golden lamp hiding behind an orange red veil
Dipped in stardust
And street hawkers sell their silvery lamps
And pots and pans of multi-coloured hues

Where time is stretchable
But there is always time
Where uninvited guests are welcome day and night

Where lemon trees line the roads
And the fruit groves

Where paper lanterns bid you good day
As they light the shop entrances
With their purples and pinks
And in fact any manner of pretty colours
Direct you into the entrance of shops
Welcoming you to try out their wares

Gouri Sadotra

The Archangel Sutras

This is India, the India of my childhood
And if I close my eyes
I can still be there

The Archangel Sutras

<u>The song of the archangel</u>

Somewhere somehow there is an archangel
singing sonorously
Singing sonorously with a voice that once
belonged to me

Isn't that what you always wanted to do?
To serenade the heavens with the songs of
angels?
Archangel

Was it the sounds of the songs of the swallows
and thrushes?
That made your stony toes tingle
temperamentally

That made you understand intelligently and
intrinsically
What music can do
In that blue hazy smoke streamed light called

Gouri Sadotra

The Archangel Sutras

dawn

To walk freely with the feet of men
And yet be able to soar in the skies like a bird
To walk in the air once more
And smell the sunshine all around

As you spread your tremendous wings in the sky
And fly up high

To command the heavens for a while
And yet still be at peace with God

Whilst lapping up the meandering silky streams
of light
That land spasmodically[81] on your stone faced
features
As you walk freely
And are truly alive once more

And I was cheering you on silently
Secretly from afar

Gouri Sadotra

The Archangel Sutras

As the very house of God is visited
Once more by the echoing repercussions of song
Sung out loud
In joyful jubilation of creation itself

Genius

What is genius?

But a measure of intelligence

An incremental scale which reaches the horizon

Then the heavens and beyond

A badge of distinction

You are so worthy

But not necessarily for what you have achieved

But for an innate quality deep within your

cerebral folds in the cortex of your head

Genius, it is potential

A potential that will carry you over

And beyond any pitfalls in your life

Order to place you at the end of mental destination

It is a talisman[82] that can protect your past present and beyond

Shielding you from all manner of disasters

Both intellectual and financial

It is a potential money earning wheel
That once you climb into and start running in
(Just like a mouse in a cage wheel)
And land you billions of zeros in your bank account
Genius is neither good nor evil
But an ability to do either
Dependent on your personality framework

The best

I took advantage of every advantage
And that made me a winner
But I was as yet a king without a crown
But my future beckoned me
For I was a child of posterity
For I lived in the future
As I understood every present day nuance
And its anticipated and unanticipated outcome
For I self willed myself to be the best
The very best

Time

Time is the most precious possession
Time is eternal, momentary, elusive, magical
Ever present
Yet something that we are unable to grasp

A concept an idea a reality and illusion it is the
past present and the future simultaneously the
snapshot of an event
Yesterday, today, or tomorrow, all at once
A potential time travellers' fantasy

A moment ever magical, or an eon long gone,
that what we cannot possess
You still don't know what it means to me
That you took time out of precious day to spend
with me

Mens rea[83]

Criminal lawyers talk about mens rea
Also known as intention
But what I realise is that there can be multiple
mens rea
Existing simultaneously
Which co-exist, coincide, and conflict
With each other
At the same time
Otherwise known as a
Conflict within the mind
Not for the action
But rather the reasons behind the action

Angels

Angels?
No worse than that
I don't even know who they are
For they
The invisible they
The all powerful
And the omnipresent they
The all seeing
And the all knowing they
They that command the heavens
Below and beyond
They that understand the nuance behind everything
They that steal the thunder from the clouds
And put it away for a rainy day
They that do everything with expressionless impassivity
They that everyone meets one day
On the exit of their final day

The Archangel Sutras

The day that their lives are extinguished forever

<u>Silence the moon</u>

And I will silence the moon
With my silvery song
With my silver tongued song

For voice is as much a part of me
As my face
Persona perfecto!
And I cannot bear to be apart from it
For even one moment

For that to happen
Would be the cause
The cause of my untimely
Too timely
Demise

Smartness in appearance

Smartness in appearance
Without intelligence
Without education
Without independent financial resources
Is a huge drain on your individual fiscal situation

Without a chance of any incremental fiscal return
Or enhancing your economic
Or romantic situation
In any respect

If this is your situation
Than it is better for you not to be preoccupied with your appearance
For it is a waste of whatever little money that you may
Or may not possess

The Archangel Sutras

And will lead you into spiralling financial
debt
Enhancing your appearance will not enhance
your IQ or your CV
Or make you more attractive to potential
employers
But your love life will improve and will
certainly get a boost

Especially if you are so amorously inclined
And sexually motivated
For possessing appearance without intellect
Is a resource without the direction of
intelligent thought

Gene bank

Who am I?
For I am nothing
No one to you
Just a gene bank
Just a holder of intellectually property rights
A person who is a collection of individual parts
That is more valuable than the whole
And are about to be auctioned of to the highest individual bidder

---

FOOTNOTES

[1] Hermes was the messenger to the ancient Greek Gods, according to ancient Greek mythology.
[2] Intergalactic means between galaxies.
[3] Orion's belt is a constellation in the night time sky.
[4] Aglow means glowing.
[5] Gossamer is a gauze or a silky like material.
[6] Silhouette means a shadow of herself.
[7] Andulusian means belonging to a region of Southern Spain.
[8] Pre-Raphaelite means a style of painting (or writing) synonymous with the Pre-Raphaelite Brotherhood.
[9] Vesuvius is a volcano in Italy that on eruption in 79 A.D. destroyed the Roman town of Pompeii.
[10] Mona Lisa is a painting by the Renaissance painter Leonardo da Vinci, she is famous for her enigmatic smile.
[11] The electromagnetic spectrum is the total spectrum of the shortest to the the longest wavelengths.
[12] Estoppel is a rule of law that stops party A from denying the truth of a statement that he has previously made. That denial must have been acted upon, (probably) to the disadvantage of, party B.

[13] Denatured means to change the nature of, often used in reference to a protein, or an enzyme.
[14] Conundrum means dilemma.
[15] Fortuitous means to be highly blessed or very lucky.
[16] Hades is the ancient Greek god of the underworld according to Greek mythology.
[17] Rapacious means greedy or destructive.
[18] Dexterity means skill.
[19] Reverberated means to resound or to echo.
[20] Myocardial infarctions means heart attacks.
[21] Subterfuge is a strategy used to hide something.
[22] Seditious means to disobey to the extent that it undermines (in this case) a person.
[23] Siphon means to drain a liquid using the principles of atmospheric pressure.
[24] Eon is an immensely long span of time that cannot be measured.
[25] A hallucination is the belief that a person is present when there is no one there.
[26] A lichen is a fungus or an algae that grow on stone walls or paths.
[27] Citadel means fortress.
[28] Elizabeth means the era of HRH Queen Elizabeth II.
[29] Labyrinth means a maze or a network of tunnels.

[30] Minotaur according to Greek mythology is a creature with the head of a bull and the body of a man.
[31] Medusa according to Greek mythology was a woman with hair made of snakes, who was so ugly to look at that she could turn you to stone.
[32] Cyclops according to Greek mythology is a giant with one eye in the middle of his forehead.
[33] Hellhounds are Satan's hounds of hell.
[34] Disheveled means to be disorganized.
[35] Mindseye according to Hinduism is the third eye that is opened during meditation.
[36] Daemon is another spelling of demon.
[37] Gnarled means rough, twisted and weather beaten in appearance.
[38] Othello is the hero of a Shakespearean tragedy and the title to the play.
[39] MacBeth, is the name of the villain in one of Shakespeare's tragedies.
[40] Embellishments means verbal ornamentation, i.e. flowery speech.
[41] Kaleidoscopic means a complex pattern of frequently changing shapes and colours.
[42] Alice in Wonderland is a book written by the author Lewis Carroll.
[43] Warrior priests means Brahmins, (in Hinduism), fighting a religious battle of good verses evil.
[44] Warrior princess, means belonging to the warrior caste according to Hinduism.

45 The burning embers are on the funeral pyre according to the last rites in Hinduism.
46 Sophocles was an ancient Greek playwright.
47 Socrates was an ancient Greek philosopher, whose discourses were written down and published by his student, Plato.
48 Byron, was a famous poet, known as Lord Byron and good friend of Shelley.
49 Wilde means Oscar Wilde, notable wit, genius and playwright.
50 Elvis Priestley.
51 Vincent Van Gogh painter most noted for his Sunflower paintings.
52 Rene Descartes, a French philosopher and mathematician.
53 Francis Bacon, an English philosopher and essayist.
54 Christopher Marlowe, an English playwright, a contemporary of William Shakespeare.
55 John Keats, an English poet.
56 The Little Mermaid, a fairy tale by Hans Christian Anderson.
57 Sycophantic means using flattery to win favour from people.
58 Cause celebre according to this poem means a famously controversial person.
59 Pantheon means a temple to the Gods.
60 An offering to God is known as prashad.
61 Shakespeare's Sister, is the name of an English all girl pop group of the 1990s.

[62] Contemporaneous means occurring in the same era.
[63] Extrapolate means to infer something unknown by deducing the known facts.
[64] A cockerel is a male hen that crows.
[65] Veracity means the truth.
[66] A nymph is a beautiful young girl.
[67] Incremental means the act of increasing.
[68] Wrestled means struggled over.
[69] Dr Jekyll is a character from the book 'The strange case of Dr Jekyll and Mr Hyde' by Robert Louis Stevenson.
[70] Mr Hyde is another character from the book, 'The strange case of Dr Jekyll and Mr Hyde' by Robert Louis Stevenson.
[71] Extrinsically, means outside.
[72] Intrinsically means inside.
[73] Frenemies are people who are simultaneously your friend and enemy.
[74] Faus pas is French for mistake.
[75] A wonderkind is German for a child prodigy.
[76] To waltz means to move in a quick and confident matter.
[77] Monsoon means the rainy season.
[78] Gulley is Hindustani for streets.
[79] Yogis are people who are masters of yoga.
[80] Arabian Nights is in reference to the book called "The thousand nights and one night".
[81] Spasmodically means in sudden brief spells.
[82] A talisman is something that is believed to protect the wearer from the forces of evil.

[83] Mens rea means intention according to Criminal law.

Printed in Great Britain
by Amazon